W9-BYH-170

Sharks

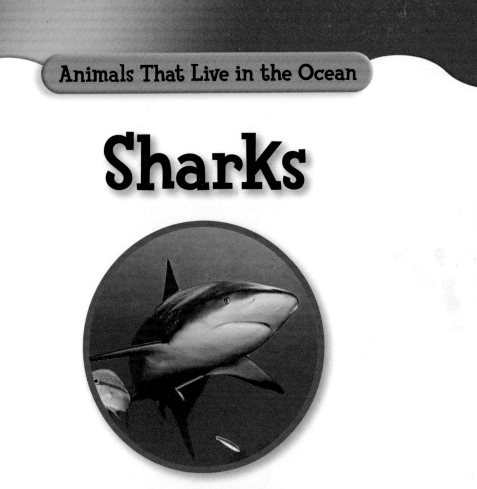

By Valerie J. Weber

Reading Consultant: Susan Nations, M.Ed.,
author/literacy coach/consultant in literacy development

Please visit our web site at www.garethstevens.com.
For a free catalog describing our list of high-quality books,
call 1-800-542-2595 (USA) or 1-800-387-3178 (Canada).
Our fax: 1-877-542-2596

Library of Congress Cataloging-in-Publication Data

Weber, Valerie.
    Sharks / by Valerie J. Weber.
        p. cm. — (Animals that live in the ocean)
    Includes bibliographical references and index.
    ISBN-10: 0-8368-9245-3 ISBN-13: 978-0-8368-9245-1 (lib. bdg.)
    ISBN-10: 0-8368-9344-1 ISBN-13: 978-0-8368-9344-1 (softcover)
    1. Sharks—Juvenile literature. I. Title.
QL638.9.W397   2008
597.3—dc22   2008009595

This edition first published in 2009 by
Weekly Reader® Books
An Imprint of Gareth Stevens Publishing
1 Reader's Digest Road
Pleasantville, NY 10570-7000 USA

Copyright © 2009 by Gareth Stevens, Inc.

Senior Managing Editor: Lisa M. Herrington
Senior Editor: Barbara Bakowski
Creative Director: Lisa Donovan
Designer: Alexandria Davis
Cover Designer: Amelia Favazza, *Studio Montage*
Photo Researcher: Diane Laska-Swanke

Photo Credits: Cover © 2007 Carson Ganci/Jupiter Images;
pp. 1, 5, 7, 9, 13, 15, 17, 19, 21 © SeaPics.com; p. 11 © Digital Vision

Printed in the United States of America

1 2 3 4 5 6 7 8 9 10 09 08

Table of Contents

Boldface words appear in the glossary.

On the Hunt

A smooth body glides through the water. A scared fish swims fast in front of it. Look out, fish! This shark is hunting!

Sharp teeth fill the shark's mouth. The shark grabs the fish tight in its strong jaws. The fish cannot get away.

Most sharks have several rows of teeth shaped like triangles. When some teeth fall out, more grow in. A great white shark can have nearly 3,000 teeth!

Shark Food

Many kinds of sharks live in the world's oceans. Most sharks eat other fish. This hammerhead shark is on the hunt for a meal.

hammerhead shark

The whale shark is the biggest shark of all. The whale shark sucks in **plankton** (PLANK-tuhn). Plankton is made up of tiny plants and animals that float in water.

whale shark

Swimming and Smelling

Sharks can swim very fast for short times. Their strong tails move them through the water. The mako (MAY-koh) is the fastest shark.

mako shark

Sharks have a great sense of smell. They can smell blood from far away. Their **nostrils** are under their **snout**.

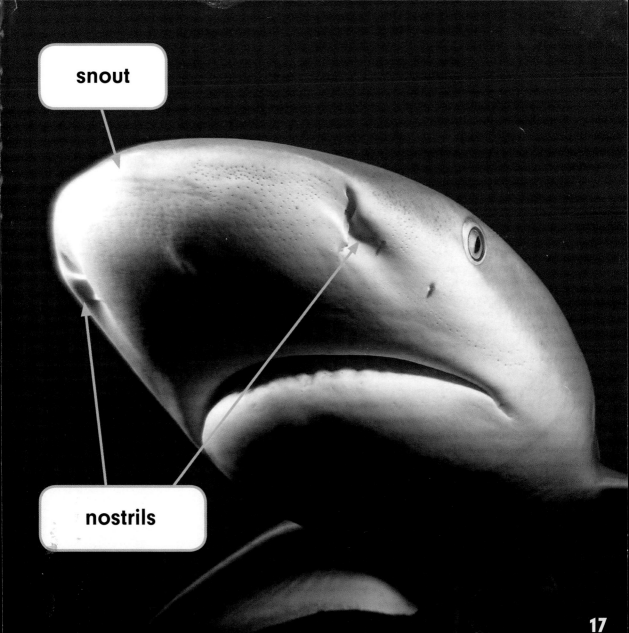

snout

nostrils

17

Baby Sharks

Most fish lay their eggs in water. Baby fish **hatch**, or come out, from these eggs. Sharks are different. Most sharks keep their eggs inside their bodies until the babies hatch.

A baby shark is ready to swim right after it hatches. It has to be. Other sharks might try to eat it!

baby shark

Glossary

hatch: to come out of an egg

nostrils: the pair of openings in the nose or snout

plankton: tiny animals and plants that float or drift in water

snout: the front part of an animal's head, including the nose

For More Information

Books

Amazing Sharks! I Can Read 2 (series).
Sarah L. Thomson (HarperCollins Publishers, 2005)

Sharks. All About Wild Animals (series)
(Gareth Stevens, 2005)

Web Sites

Sharks at Enchanted Learning
www.enchantedlearning.com/subjects/sharks/index.html
Click on links to find out about the sharks that swim the world's oceans.

Shedd Aquarium: Sharks
www.sheddaquarium.org/sea/guide_eng.cfm?cat_id=1
Click on links to learn more about various kinds of sharks.

Index

About the Author

A writer and editor for 25 years, Valerie Weber especially loves working in children's publishing. The variety of topics is endless, from weird animals to making movies. It is her privilege to try to engage children in their world through books.